D0513861

Sleepover Party

DK

DK | Penguin Random House

Senior Designer Wendy Bartlet
Project Editor Laura Palosuo
Designers Eleanor Bates, Charlotte Bull, Rachael Hare
Assistant Editor Sophia Danielsson-Waters
Photographer Dave King
Illustrator Rachael Hare
Jacket Designer Wendy Bartlet
Pre-production Andy Hilliard, Dragana Puvacic
Producer Georgina Russell
Creative Technical Support Sonia Charbonnier
Managing Editor Penny Smith
Managing Art Editor Gemma Glover
Art Director Jane Bull
Publisher Mary Ling

First published in Great Britain in 2016 by
Dorling Kindersley Limited
80 Strand, London WC2R 0RL

Copyright © 2016 Dorling Kindersley Limited
A Penguin Random House Company

10 9 8 7 6 5 4 3 2 1

001–285434– February/2016

All rights reserved.
No part of this publication may be reproduced, stored in or introduced into a
retrieval system, or transmitted, in any form, or by any means (electronic,
mechanical, photocopying, recording, or otherwise), without the prior written
permission of the copyright owner.

A CIP catalogue record for this book is available from the British Library.

ISBN: 978-0-2412-3103-6

Printed and bound in China by RR Donnelley

All images © Dorling Kindersley Limited
For further information see: www.dkimages.com

A WORLD OF IDEAS
SEE ALL THERE IS TO KNOW

www.dk.com

SAFETY

This book is packed with things to do – some are simple, while others are more tricky. We hope you enjoy this book, but please be sensible and safe. **Tell an adult before you do any of the projects, carefully read all the instructions, and seek help whenever you need it**, especially for **cooking, cutting, and sewing**. Whenever you see:

⚠

please ask an adult for help. The publisher cannot take responsibility for the outcome, injury, loss, damage, or mess that occurs as a result of you attempting any of the activities in this book.

Contents

Party planner

All the best parties need a bit of prepping. Have a good think, talk to an adult, and make a list. Use the notes on this page to help you plan.

Invitations

4

Party Ideas

Will your party have a theme? We've got some great ideas and inspiration (pages 6–15). Will you choose a marvellous movie night or pamper your friends with a super spa bash?

Food and Drink

Start by checking if there are any foods your guests can't eat. Talk to an adult to sort out ideas for the main meal and breakfast. Other things to think about are drinks, snacks, and perhaps a midnight feast!

Activities

It's good to have some activities prepared just in case you're stuck for what to do. Luckily, this book has loads of ideas that'll entertain everyone!

Sleeping

Where will your guests sleep? Tell them in advance if they need to bring a sleeping bag, pillow, or duvet. Make a plan before the party starts, so you don't have to figure out arrangements when you're all tired.

Party Bags

Giving out party bags is a great way to thank your guests for coming. Look on pages 74–75 for inspiration on what to put inside.

Party idea: Pamper party

A luxurious pamper party is a great way to unwind, relax, and treat your friends. Hang up lovely decorations, put on soothing music, and become the best spa in town!

Find out how to make these hanging heart decorations on page 76. You can also use the heart templates for bunting.

A DIY foot spa is super soothing for your soles.

Pamper your nails

No spa party is complete without a manicure. Head to pages 16-17 for nail art inspiration. You could also do pedicures after you've tried the foot spa on pages 22-23.

How to make pom-pom decorations

⚠️

1 Fold a few sheets of tissue paper back and forth, concertina-style.

2 Cut off the concertina's corners. Tie thread around it.

3 Separate and fluff out the layers on either side.

Hang up paper pom-poms for a pretty and sophisticated look.

Fruity facials (pages 18-19) and comfy eye masks (pages 38-39) are pamper party essentials!

Invitations

You can use the eye mask template on page 78 for your spa sleepover invitations.

Use plainer paper on the front, and stick patterned paper on the back.

Pamper Party

To:
Place:
Time:
Date:

Use colourful envelopes to complement your invites.

Party idea: Campout

Bring the outdoors inside with your own crazy, cool camping party. Set up a pretend campfire as the centre of the action, tell stories, play games, and giggle the whole night long!

Send invites that guests can open like a tent!

Put up signs for rooms! The loo can be the "outhouse". The kitchen can be the "picnic area".

Prepare a scavenger hunt! Compile a list of things guests need to find. The first person to get them all wins!

For bunting, cut out diamonds from a fabric. Fold them over a ribbon to make triangle shapes. Staple to secure.

Campout invitations

Copy the template on page 77 onto card.

Cut along this line.

Fold out along the dotted lines.

Glue the tent sides onto a piece of coloured card.

The flaps fold out here!

Write details on the card underneath the flaps.

8

Mini teepees

You may need to get an adult to help you as this is quite fiddly. Hold 5 garden canes together, and tie them at the top. Pull the bottom of the canes out to make a circle. Next, hang a sheet or duvet around the canes, and tie at the top to secure.

Use pegs to hold open the front flaps.

Tie the canes with string.

Sit in a circle and tell spooky stories!

There's no need to make a real fire – this one's made of yellow and red tissue paper, logs, and stones.

Try making dream catchers on pages 42-43.

9

Party idea: Fashion

If you love clothes, crafting, and customizing, a super-stylish fashion-themed party will be just up your street. Get creative with your hair, outfits, and shoes, then you're ready to strut your stuff!

Bling Rings

Make these funky rings (pages 50-51). Choose colours that match your outfits.

Find out how to make these lovely tutus on pages 56-57.

Don't forget to take the quiz on pages 34-35 to find out what type of fashionista you are!

Invitations

For fashionable invites, copy the handbag template on page 77 onto pretty card.

Fashion Sleepover

Write all your party information on the front.

How to make chains

Patterned paper-chain decorations work well for a fancy, fashion theme.

⚠️ **1**
Cut lots of strips of different patterned paper, 3cm (1in) wide, and 30cm (12in) long.

2
To make a loop, place two strips on top of each other, patterned sides facing out. Staple the ends together.

3
Keep making loops, securing each one by stapling together through the previous loop. Make the chain as long as you like.

Make these funky raggedy bangles on pages 46-47.

Revamp a pair of flip-flops! For inspiration, head to pages 62-63.

Hair Styling

You can't have a fashion party without hair styling! Learn how to create different styles (pages 20-21), or create your own clip-in hair wraps (pages 60-61).

Party idea: Pop star

You don't have to love singing to be a pop star. It's all about the attitude! Put up funky decorations, play some good music, and have a karaoke or jam session!

Hang up blank CDs for glitzy decorations, or use them as coasters.

VIP pass

VIP invitations

Make your invites look like VIP passes! Write the party details on card, make a hole in the top, and add a long ribbon. Give these to your guests to hang around their necks. Only let them in if they show their passes!

Rocking kicks

Want that ultimate rock star look? Jazz up your favourite plain canvas trainers (pages 58-59) to add a cool step to your dance routines.

Nibble on perfect pizzas using the recipe on pages 70-71.

For rock-star bunting, use the templates on page 79. Gold, glittery card looks amazing.

Keep the music playing with loads of tunes you all like, and some sing-along classics.

You'll look like cool pop stars sipping on scrummy mocktails (pages 66-67).

Sip on your mocktails through funky straws. Find decoration templates on page 79.

13

Party idea: Movie night

Making films the main feature of your party is a totally top idea. They are brilliant to watch – and there are so many fun film activities you can do, plus ways to set the scene. And... action!

Use the frames from pages 26-27 to take film star photos.

INVITATION

TO ....

DATE ....

Nothing says "the movies" more than invites styled to look like clapperboards!

For bunting, find some stars and stripes paper, cut out diamonds, and then fold over a long piece of ribbon. Staple to secure in place.

Go to pages 68-69 to find a great way to make popcorn. How can you have a film night without it?

Candy bangles

Sit and watch films with candy bangles on your wrists (pages 52-53). Try not to finish them before the movie's over!

Lay out a "red carpet" for your guests at the entrance of your home.

Nail art

1 Paint two large dots, then add a smaller one underneath.

2 Smooth the sides to create a pretty heart shape.

Simple dots work best when you use contrasting colours.

Pretty heart

Polka dots

2 Use another colour to add a dot in the middle of the daisy.

Crazy daisy

1 Make five equal dots in a circle. Let dry.

It's so much fun to give someone a manicure! Paint a base coat first and let dry. Then try out these pretty designs. And remember to keep the grown-ups happy – don't spill your varnish on your clothes, carpets, or furniture!

1
Before you start, make sure your hands are clean. Paint your first base coat, and let it dry. Apply a few base coats in this way.

Base coat

1 Use a pink base coat, then add black dots.

Sweet strawberry

Lovely ladybird

2 When dry, add a spiky green pattern for the leaves.

1 Paint a black semicircle and a line on a red base. Let dry.

2 Add spots and two white dots for eyes. When dry, add pupils.

1 Paint one large circle and two small dots for the ears. Let dry.

2 Paint a semicircle in a lighter colour. When dry, add eyes and nose.

Cuddly bear

Vary dots in different sizes for a fun, bold look.

Spots in a row

Stuff you'll need!
: Non-toxic, peel-off nail varnish
: Cocktail sticks

Magic stick!

2
Use the cocktail stick for an easy way to make dots or patterns. Dip it in varnish and touch it lightly to the nail.

1 Paint two big white dots for the eyes.

Eye see you!

2 When dry, add black pupils inside the white dots.

Cute bunny

Puppy paw

1 Paint a semicircle on the bottom half of the nail, then add oval ears.

2 When dry, paint on eyes and a nose with a different colour.

Try different sized dots for a cute puppy paw print.

Fruity facials

Turns out fruit isn't just yummy in your tummy – it's great for your skin, too! These facials are a little luxury that will make you all feel pampered. Leave for 10-20 minutes, then rinse off with warm water.

Strawberries & cream

Avocado & lime

How much?
These recipes make enough for one face mask. Multiply the quantities by the number of guests you have.

Banana & honey

Pop cucumber slices over your eyes for that super spa feeling.

Honey makes your skin feel silky smooth.

Mash together!

- 2-3 strawberries
- I tbsp of double cream
- I tsp of honey

Strawberries boost skin radiance.

Lime juice is good for balancing oily skin.

Avocados are great skin conditioners.

Mash together!

- ½ small avocado
- I tbsp of yoghurt
- A squeeze of lime juice

Ripe bananas are lovely moisturisers.

Mash together!

- I ripe banana
- I tsp of honey
- A squeeze of lemon juice

Lemon juice helps to make your skin less shiny.

Hair flair

It's much more fun to create hairstyles with friends than on your own. Here are some ideas to get you started.

Twisted ponytail

1 Divide the hair into two sections. Twist one section tightly. Don't let go!

2 Now twist the other section in the same way.

3 Bring both sections together and twist them around each other. Secure with a hair elastic or ribbon.

Three-way plait

1 Divide the hair into three even sections. Plait each section and secure the ends.

A flower hides the hair elastics!

2 Plait the three sections together to make a larger plait.

Hair bow

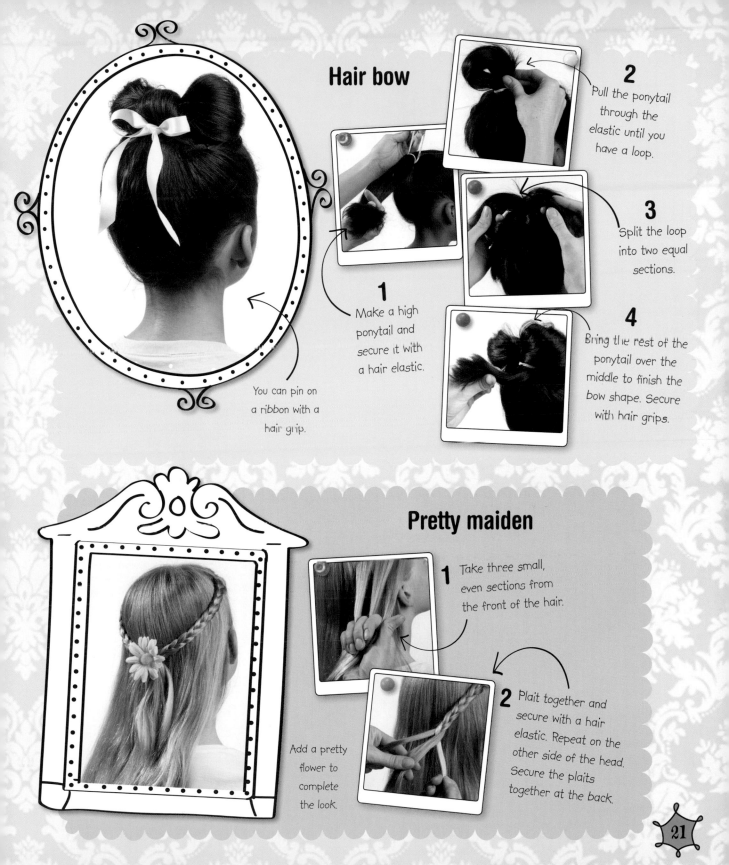

1 Make a high ponytail and secure it with a hair elastic.

2 Pull the ponytail through the elastic until you have a loop.

3 Split the loop into two equal sections.

4 Bring the rest of the ponytail over the middle to finish the bow shape. Secure with hair grips.

You can pin on a ribbon with a hair grip.

Pretty maiden

1 Take three small, even sections from the front of the hair.

2 Plait together and secure with a hair elastic. Repeat on the other side of the head. Secure the plaits together at the back.

Add a pretty flower to complete the look.

Foot soak spa

Stuff you'll need!

- 10 tbsp of Epsom salts
- 2 tbsp bicarbonate of soda
- 2 drops of essential oils
- Rose petals

Makes enough for 12!

Rose petals look pretty and can help to soothe dry skin.

Running, dancing, jumping, we're always on our feet....

...so they deserve some TLC! Pamper your guests with your own DIY foot soak.

1

Measure the Epsom salts into a bowl, and then add the bicarbonate of soda.

2

Add 2 drops of essential oils to make the foot soak smell lovely.

3

Stir it all together. Your homemade foot soak mix is now ready.

4

To use, fill a bowl with warm water for each person and add 1 tbsp of the mixture to each bowl.

Make sure the bowl is big enough to fit your feet in.

5

Top with rose petals. Soak your feet for 10 minutes, then rinse and dry. Bliss!

What type of friend are you?

Take this quiz to find out.

Are you the kind of friend who's always looking after others, the jokey one who loves to laugh, or the one who organises exciting activities?

Tell her straight away – cringe!

Your friend has toilet roll stuck to her shoe! You...

It doesn't matter as long as we spend time together.

Tell her, after a lot of giggling!

Start
What do you do on a day out with your friends?

Something fun, like going to the cinema or going shopping.

Test what type of friend you are!

Your friend is feeling sad. You...

Caring & kind

There's a new student at school and she seems quite shy. What do you do?

Say something friendly and show her around.

You look after your friends and hate to see anyone sad. You and your close friends share everything.

Apologise and give her a hug.

Tell a funny story to put her at ease.

Silly & fun

You know loads of jokes and love to make your friends laugh. They count on you to bring the fun – whatever the occasion.

You can't go to your friend's birthday party! You...

Sit with her and have a cosy chat.

Try and arrange something to do when you're both free.

The joker – you love a giggle and a good time.

Active & social

Take her out and try to make her laugh.

In a group of friends you are...

The organiser. You love getting everyone together.

You love doing things with the people you like the most. You are always suggesting new activities and like to invite everyone along.

25

You've been framed!

With just a camera and some props you can set up an at-home photo booth and take these fun "framed" photos. Give everyone a turn to pose and try out their sweetest smile – and silliest face.

Stuff you'll need!

- Frame – use an old picture frame or draw a frame on cardboard, colour it in, and cut it out. ⚠
- Funny hats, colourful sunglasses, feather boas, and any other accessories you can think of.
- A camera or a camera phone.

Giggly games

Not many parties can be planned with absolute military precision, so there may be a moment or two when you're stuck for what to do next. But don't worry – we have some great game ideas!

Who am I?

Get everyone to sit in a circle and secretly write the name of a famous person on a sticky note. Each person then sticks their note onto the forehead of the person sitting next to them (without letting that person see what's on the note). Everyone then takes turns to ask questions with "yes" or "no" answers to work out who they are.

The laughing game

Each person goes around in a circle and has to say either "Hee", "Ha", or "Ho". Anyone who starts laughing is knocked out, until you have one (stony-faced) champion remaining!

Hairdo dash

Split your guests into pairs, and get each pair to sit next to each other in a circle. Put lots of cheap hair accessories where everyone can reach them and set a five-minute time limit. The pairs have to grab what they can and style each other's hair before the time's up. Ask a grown up to judge the winner.

Truth or dare

The classic sleepover party game! Each person has to choose whether to answer a "truth" or do a "dare". Try and come up with a good question that the person must reveal the truth about, or something funny to do as a dare!

What's that song?

Play a song you think your guests will recognise. The first guest to correctly guess the song title gets a point, plus an extra point if they name the singer. Keep playing different songs until someone has 10 points.

Musical statues

Put on music and get everyone to dance. Pause the music at random points. Suddenly everyone must stand as still as a statue, in the position they were in when the music stopped. If you wobble, you're out! Keep playing until there's a winner.

Spin the nail varnish bottle

Everyone sits in a circle holding a varnish (use non-toxic, peel-off varnishes in different colours). Take turns spinning a varnish in the middle (make sure the lid's on tight!). The person the varnish points to has to paint one nail of each person with their colour. Continue until you have a full manicure. The person whose colour was used most wins!

Guess the secret

Everybody has to write down something about themselves that they think the others wouldn't know, and then put the notes (folded-up) in a bowl. One person at a time has to pull out a note, then read it aloud. Everyone has to try and guess whose secret it is!

29

Zodiac pals

Some people think your star sign may influence your personality. Find your sign on these pages – does the description match the type of friend you are?

Sagittarius
22 November – 21 December

Perfect pals with: *Aries, Aquarius, Leo, Libra.* Sagittarians are bubbly, happy, and full of fun. They are very lively and always want to try new things.

Capricorn
22 December – 19 January

Perfect pals with: *Pisces, Scorpio, Taurus, Virgo.* Capricorns are practical, sensible friends. They're wise, so they're good to go to for advice.

Scorpio
23 October – 21 November

Perfect pals with: *Cancer, Capricorn, Pisces, Virgo.* It's hard to be bored with a Scorpio. They're fun, passionate, and like to make sure that their friends are okay.

Libra
23 September – 22 October

Perfect pals with: *Aquarius, Gemini, Leo, Sagittarius.* If you're having trouble, ask a Libra for advice. Librans are calm, kind, and fair. They try to understand every point of view.

Virgo
23 August – 22 September

Perfect pals with: *Capricorn, Scorpio, Taurus.* Go to a Virgo when you need honest advice. They always want to help out their friends.

Leo
23 July – 22 August

Perfect pals with: *Aries, Libra, Gemini, Sagittarius.* Leos are warm and bubbly. They're generally leaders of groups, just like the lion – their symbol.

Garnet

Turquoise

Topaz

Opal

Sapphire

Peridot

Aquarius

20 January – 18 February

Perfect pals with: Aries, Gemini, Libra, Sagittarius. Aquarians are imaginative and open-minded. They like coming up with quirky ideas.

Amethyst

Aquamarine

Diamond

Emerald

Pearl

Ruby

Birthstones

Each zodiac sign is represented by at least one birthstone. Look in the middle of the page to see what yours is – wearing it may bring you luck!

Pisces

19 February – 20 March

Perfect pals with: Capricorn, Cancer, Scorpio, Taurus. Pisceans are kind, creative, and artistic – and may like to dance, paint, or sing!

Aries

21 March – 19 April

Perfect pals with: Aquarius, Gemini, Leo, Sagittarius. Aries are the life and soul of a party. They're friendly and upbeat, but also like to be independent.

Taurus

20 April – 20 May

Perfect pals with: Cancer, Capricorn, Pisces, Virgo. Taureans are down-to-earth and dependable. They're always up for doing fun things – especially if it involves fine food!

Gemini

21 May – 20 June

Perfect pals with: Aries, Aquarius, Leo, Libra. Geminis are charming and lively. They find it easy to get on with different groups of people.

Cancer

21 June – 22 July

Perfect pals with: Pisces, Scorpio, Taurus, Virgo. At first it might be hard to get to know a Cancer. But they're actually loving and caring friends.

Fortune tellers

You don't need magical powers to predict the future – a fortune teller does it for you! Try and invent hilarious fortunes that'll make you all giggle.

How many kids will I have – one, five, or 17!?

What will I be when I grow up – an actor, a pilot, a scientist, or a teacher?

Will I live in a castle, a mansion, a cottage, or a shack?

How to Play

Pick a colour from the outside of the fortune teller, for instance "red" – three letters.

Open the fortune teller once for each letter – sideways, up and down, sideways again.

Pick a number. Open the fortune teller that many times.

Choose another number and open the flap to reveal your fortune!

Stuff you'll need!

- Square piece of paper
- Colouring pens

Fold the paper in half, top to bottom. Make a firm crease and unfold.

Fold again, this time from side to side, and unfold.

Fold a corner into the centre and crease it down.

Do this again with each of the other corners.

Turn the square over. Fold a corner into the centre.

Repeat with the other three corners, creasing each one firmly.

Fold the square in half, top to bottom. Make a crease and unfold.

Fold again, side to side this time, then unfold.

Put your thumb and index fingers into the pockets and pick up the fortune teller.

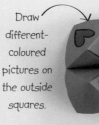

Draw different-coloured pictures on the outside squares.

Write numbers on all the inside triangles.

It should look like this! Now fill in the outside squares and inside triangles.

Open the inside flaps and write on the fortunes.

33

What type of fashionista are you?

Are you the sporty, wild, or glamorous type?

You have great taste and wear clothes that really suit you. But what fashion category do you fit into? Take this quiz to find out!

Going on a bike ride.

Wear something you feel happy and confident in.

What sounds like more fun?

Start

You're going to the school disco. You...

Going shopping.

Energetic and friendly.

Wear something quirky or glitzy – you love to sparkle!

Your friends would describe you as...

Trendy and hip.

34

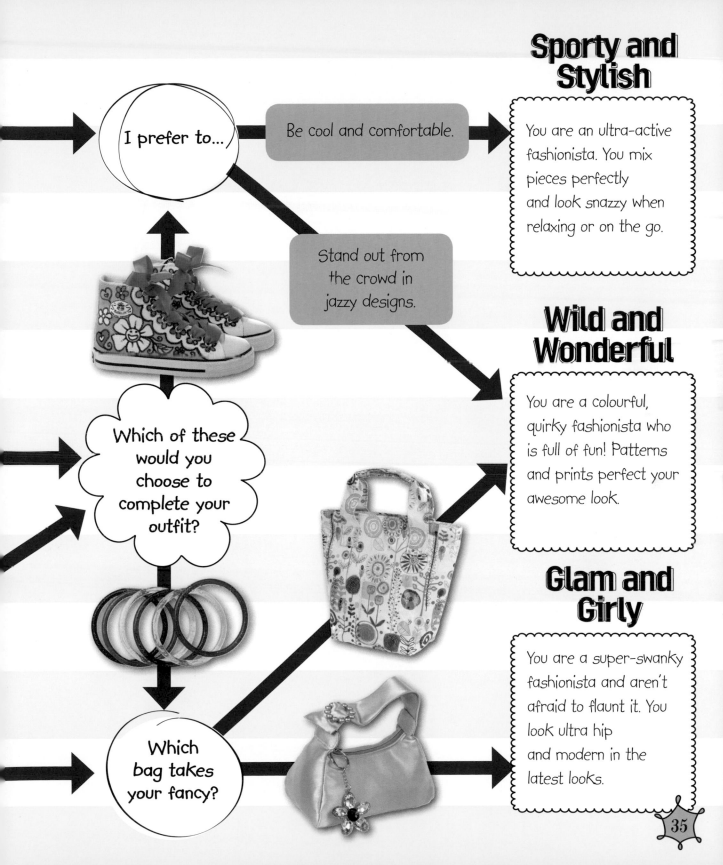

Sporty and Stylish

I prefer to...

Be cool and comfortable.

You are an ultra-active fashionista. You mix pieces perfectly and look snazzy when relaxing or on the go.

Stand out from the crowd in jazzy designs.

Wild and Wonderful

Which of these would you choose to complete your outfit?

You are a colourful, quirky fashionista who is full of fun! Patterns and prints perfect your awesome look.

Glam and Girly

Which bag takes your fancy?

You are a super-swanky fashionista and aren't afraid to flaunt it. You look ultra hip and modern in the latest looks.

Flower power hairbands

Ribbons add that finishing touch.

Put the flowers at a jaunty angle.

Use black and red tissue paper for poppies.

36

Hairbands add fun and glamour to any outfit. These tissue paper delights are easy to make, and you and your friends can wear them as soon as you're done!

Stuff you'll need!

- Coloured tissue paper
- Scissors
- Pipe cleaners
- Plain hairband for each person
- Ribbon

1

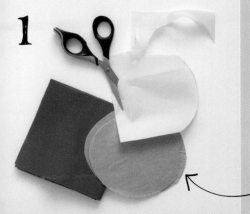

Fold the tissue paper so that it's about 10 layers thick. Cut a circle through all the layers. Do the same with all the tissue paper colours you want to use, making sure your circles are the same size. ⚠️

3

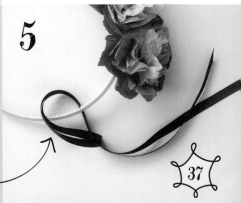

Firmly twist the pipe cleaner around the pinched base until it's secure. Then, starting from the middle, separate out each layer of tissue paper. Gently scrunch and crinkle the layers to create full and pretty petals.

2

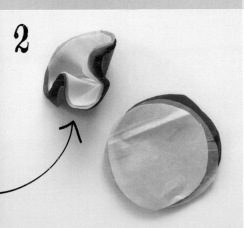

4

⚠️ Attach the flowers by twisting the ends of the pipe cleaner around the hairband. Cut off any excess.

Fold the ribbon in half and place it over the hairband. Bring the ends through the loop to secure.

5

Enchanting eye masks

Can't sleep? A good way to get some shut-eye is to wear a comfy mask that blocks out the outside world. This fashionable one is fun to make with friends!

Stuff you'll need!

- Paper, pencil, and scissors
- Wadding
- Coloured felt
- Fabric pen, gems and fabric glue
- Pins, embroidery needle and thread
- Elastic (length to fit your head)

1 Trace the template on page 78 onto paper and cut it out. Place it on the wadding and cut around the template with scissors.

You can trim the wadding to make it a bit smaller than the felt.

Choose a colour of felt that your fabric pen will show up on.

2 Use the paper template to cut out two pieces of felt for the front and back of the mask. Put the wadding between the two pieces of felt, and pin all three layers together..

3

With an adult's help, thread your needle, knot the end, and sew around the edges of the mask.

4

Stitch the ends of the elastic to the back of the mask. It's now ready to decorate! Use the fabric pen (keep it away from your clothes and any furniture), then stick on the gems with fabric glue.

Embellish the mask with pretty gems.

Felt fun

These felty wonders are great for just about anything – tie them to your bag, hang them up as decorations, or pin them to your jacket. The possibilities are endless, so let your imagination run wild!

⚠️ Trace the templates on page 78 onto paper (you can choose hearts or flowers). Cut out the templates and pin each one to a different-coloured piece of felt. Then carefully cut around each template.

1

Stuff you'll need!

- Paper
- Felt squares in different colours
- Pins and scissors
- Buttons in different colours
- Needle and thread
- Ribbons

2

Make a pile of your shapes with the smallest ones on top. Choose two or three buttons and stack them on the front. **With the help of an adult**, thread your needle and knot the end of your thread. ⚠️

3

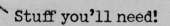

Holding it all together, start at the back and pass the needle and thread through all the layers and one set of button holes, then go back through the other button holes. Do this a few times, then make a knot at the back. ⚠️

Sew a ribbon to the back to hang up your decoration.

4

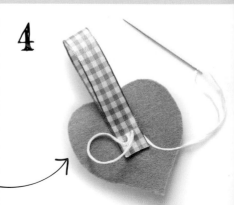

40

Dream catchers

Stuff you'll need!

- Embroidery hoop or hoop made from craft wire
- Ribbon
- Glue
- Embroidery thread or string
- Beads and feathers for decoration

Native Americans make dream catchers to catch bad dreams. They are perfect for sleepovers. Make one together and hang it in your bedroom.

You can use craft wire to make a hoop.

1

Start by wrapping the hoop with the ribbon. Secure with a little glue at both ends.

2

Knot one end of the thread tightly around the hoop.

3

Loop the thread around the hoop as shown. Pull the thread to tighten it.

4

Continue around the hoop, making evenly-spaced loops until you get back to the start knot.

5

Start a second round, this time making loops around the centres of the sections.

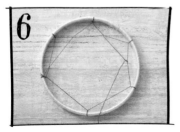

6

Carry on until you finish the second round. Try to keep the thread tight.

7

Continue making rounds in this way, and thread on beads as you work towards the middle.

8

When you reach the middle, secure with a knot. Cut off the extra thread.

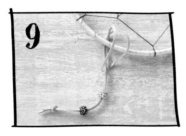

9

Take a length of string, double it over, and thread on beads. Knot the end. Loop over the hoop to attach.

10

Repeat step 9 four more times. Push feathers into the bead holes – pack tightly so they won't fall out.

To hang up your dream catcher, attach thread or string to the top and add on beads.

What's your ideal fancy dress costume?

What are you destined to become next?

If you're stuck on deciding on a costume, give this quick quiz a go. You'll find out what will suit your personality best.

Start
You are somewhere new with lots of people you have never met before. What do you do first?

Go and chat to people.

Speak to animals.

Be able to fly.

Which of these magical powers would you most like to have? To...

You are more suited for a life in...

What sounds like more fun?

An enchanted forest.

The wide, open prairies.

Horse riding.

Colourful Fairy

You are sugary sweet and super friendly. Pop on a pair of wings, get your wand ready, and ta-da – a magical transformation right before your eyes!

Wild West Hero

Yee-haw! Go lasso your hat, bandanna, and checked shirt and let's head on down to the rodeo, Partner!

44

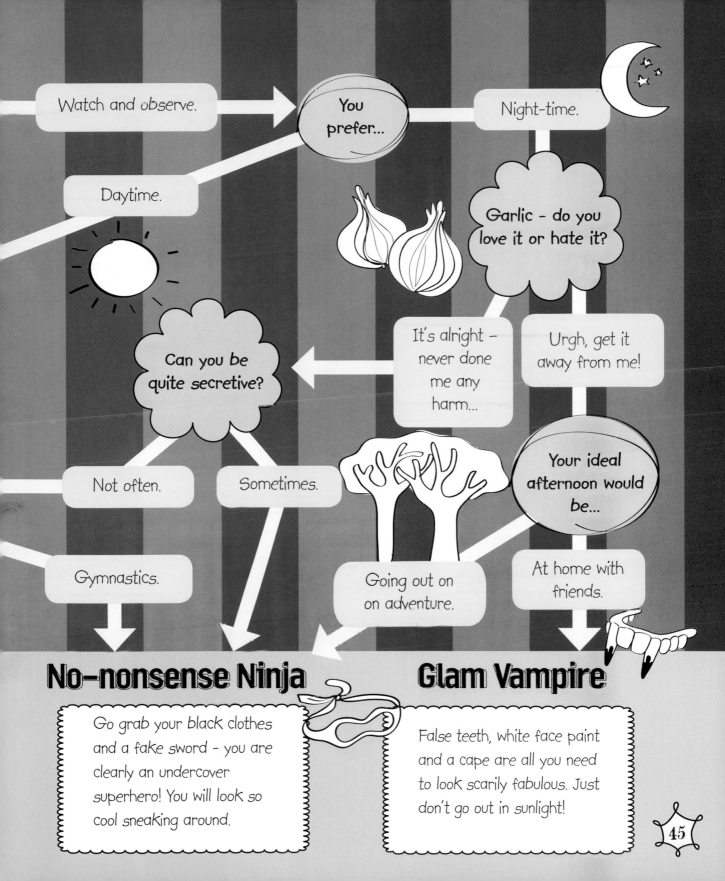

Watch and observe.

You prefer...

Night-time.

Daytime.

Garlic - do you love it or hate it?

Can you be quite secretive?

It's alright – never done me any harm...

Urgh, get it away from me!

Not often.

Sometimes.

Your ideal afternoon would be...

Gymnastics.

Going out on on adventure.

At home with friends.

No-nonsense Ninja

Go grab your black clothes and a fake sword - you are clearly an undercover superhero! You will look so cool sneaking around.

Glam Vampire

False teeth, white face paint and a cape are all you need to look scarily fabulous. Just don't go out in sunlight!

Raggedy bangles

Jangly bracelets add a pretty decoration to your wrist, and show off your funky fashion sense. So why not make your own super easy beady bangles?

Stuff you'll need!
- Cotton fabric and scissors
- Beads – large and small
- Elastic thread
- Darning needle (if you want)

1

Make a small snip into the cotton with the scissors, then pull off a strip with your hands so the sides are ragged. Make around 6 strips for each bracelet.

Mix different cotton fabrics for a funky effect.

2

Thread beads onto the elastic, alternating large and small ones. You can do this with your hands, or **ask an adult** to help you thread them with a darning needle.

3

When the bracelet is long enough to fit comfortably around your wrist, tie the ends in a knot. Then tie the ragged strips over the elastic between the beads.

Lucky charms

These sweet charms look good enough to eat! You can make them into keyrings or matching necklaces for everyone.

Stuff you'll need!

- Oven-bake polymer clay
- Wooden modelling tool
- Beads for decoration
- Small screw-eyes
- Ribbons or keyrings

Make a tiny doughnut by sticking a thin disk on a thick one. Then make the hole with your modelling tool.

1 To make a tiny cupcake, shape the clay into three 2cm (³/₄in) balls for the cake, case, and icing. Make another smaller ball to go on top.

2 Shape the case so it's smaller at the top and larger on the bottom. Flatten each end. Use a modelling tool to make side folds as shown.

3 Flatten the top and bottom of the cake, making sure it's wider than your case. Press the case onto your cake.

4 Roll the icing into a long sausage, making it smaller towards one end. Then starting at the narrow end, shape it into a swirl.

For a hamburger, make three thick disks for the meat and buns. Don't forget the cheese and lettuce!

You can use real sprinkles to decorate your sweet creations!

5 Turn your cake and case the right way up. Firmly attach the icing to the top of the cake.

6 Press beads into the icing for decoration. Then pop the small ball of clay on the top so it looks like a cherry.

7 Press the screw-eye into the top. **Ask an adult** to bake your charm in the oven according to the clay manufacturer's instructions.

8 Make sure your charm has cooled down. Then attach a pretty ribbon or a keyring to the screw-eye.

Rings and things

Stuff you'll need!

- Assorted beads
- Craft wire
- Pliers to help you hold and twist the wire.
- Scissors

Twisty bead ring

Bead band rings

Try out lots of colour combinations!

Making these bling rings is an awesome party activity that lets everyone get creative, colourful, and crafty. Even better – guests can take them home afterwards!

How to make a twisty bead ring

1 Thread a big bead onto a 12cm (5in) length of wire. Twist the wire around the bead to hold it in place.

2 Thread smaller beads onto the wire until you're about 2cm (¾in) from the end.

3 Add another big bead to the end, then wind the wire around the bead.

4 Snip off any excess wire. Wrap the ring around your finger to get the right fit.

How to make a bead band ring

1 Thread one large bead onto a 25cm (10in) length of wire. Add a small bead either side.

2 Centre the beads on the wire, then pop another large bead on one side.

3 Feed the other end of the wire back through the same bead, in the other direction.

4 Pull both ends of the wire to close the gap, then add two more small beads.

5 Keep repeating steps 2-4 until the ring fits around your finger.

6 To finish off, bring the end of the wire back through the bead you started with.

7 Feed the other end of the wire through this bead too, but in the opposite direction.

8 Tighten, and twist the wire around the bead to secure. Snip off the extra wire.

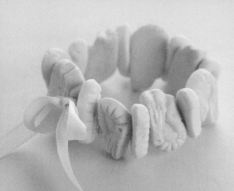

Stuff you'll need!

- Ribbon (enough to wrap around your wrist and a little extra for the bow)
- Sweets with holes or soft sweets
- Scissors
- Needle and thread (for soft sweets without holes)

⚠️

With an adult's help, you could use a needle and thread to make a bracelet from soft sweets that don't have holes.

Candy bangles

These super sweet bracelets couldn't be easier to make. Just thread a ribbon through the centre of your sweets, tie it on your wrist, make a bow – and ta-da! (Just try not to eat it straight away.)

What's your inner animal?

What's the animal inside YOU?

Are you a friendly dolphin, a cool cat or a wise owl? Take this quiz to find out which cute critter you secretly are....

2

Do you like swimming?
A: You love it - you're basically a fish!
B: You'll paddle – and keep your hair dry!
C: No! You'd rather sit by the water and watch the world go by.

1

You're going to the cinema. What type of film do you choose?
A: A comedy – you love a good giggle.
B: An old black-and-white film – you're very sophisticated, you see.
C: A historical drama where all the characters are dressed up.

Mostly A's: Dolphin

You're a cheerful, energetic dolphin. You make everything fun and you love to laugh. Even the grumpiest person can't be angry when you're around!

Most B's: Cat

You're an independent, cool cat. You know what suits you and you stick with it. Your special friends love you because you're so charming.

3

You generally prefer to hang out with...
A: A large group of friends.
B: One friend who is important to you.
C: A few close friends.

4

Someone asks you to clean your room. What do you do?
A: You only do a bit of tidying – you'd rather go out and play.
B: You don't do it – what a ridiculous question!
C: You do it quickly, but then have a nice nap.

5

What would you rather do for fun with friends?
A: Go outside and play games.
B: Do something a bit different, such as rock climbing or abstract painting.
C: Play board games at home.

Mostly C's: Owl

You're a clever and wise owl. You're a great listener with smart and sensible ideas. People turn to you when they need advice as you'll always stay calm, and have something helpful to say.

55

No-sew tutus

Hey there, young stars-to-be! You should totally dance and prance about the house wearing these funky tutus. They're just great for dressing up and putting on a show!

Stuff you'll need!

- 2 metres (6½ft) tulle fabric
- Ribbon
- Scissors

1 Cut a long length of ribbon for the waistband. Cut the tulle into strips that are 12cm (5in) wide and at least 1 metre (3ft) long. Fold each strip in half, place it over the ribbon, and bring the ends through the loop to secure.

2

Keep adding strips of tulle to the ribbon. Shuffle them together to make the tutu full and fluffy. For that extra something, you can add lengths of ribbon – or even different coloured tulle – at various points as you go along.

3

When you've knotted enough material around the ribbon waistband, tie the two ends together around your waist. Make a pretty bow and snip off any excess.

Transform your trainers

Fed up of plain, dull footwear? Well, here's a fun way to get creative and add a colourful kick to some boring, bland shoes!

Stuff you'll need!

- Pair of clean canvas trainers
- Pencil and rubber
- Black and coloured fabric marker pens
- Ribbon (if you want)

1

Remove the laces from your canvas trainers. Your first job is to draw your design. Use a pencil so you can rub out any mistakes. You can also plan your design on paper before you start.

You can rub out mistakes at this stage.

2

Get out your black fabric marker and draw over the outlines of your design. Remember to always take care with your marker pens. Keep them away from your clothes and the furniture because they do stain!

58

3

Once you have drawn your outline design, it's time to get colourful! Using your coloured markers, carefully colour in your trainers. You can be as creative as you want. Go colour mad or just use a couple of colours – it's up to you.

4

As a finishing touch, why not add some colourful ribbon for new laces? You could also use wool or cord.

Hair wraps

Hair wraps look cool and are so simple to make. Our clever wraps clip in and out, so you can try loads of styles!

Starting off

Take several lengths of thread about 1m (3ft) long. Loop them through a safety pin so that they are doubled over.

Tie a knot at the top of your threads. You're now ready to start making bands of colour and spirals in any order you like!

One-colour band

Take a couple of the threads that are one colour, and wrap them tightly around the other threads.

Keep wrapping until your first band is 3cm (1in) long. Then secure it by pulling the threads through the last wrap.

Stuff you'll need!

- Embroidery thread
- Safety pin
- Beads
- Hair clips

⚠️ Attach the safety pin to a pillow to keep the wraps steady and your hands free.

60

Single spiral

To make a spiral, pull out one or two threads. Wrap around with another colour to make a 3cm (1in) band.

Now take the threads you left at the top, and spiral them down over the top of the band.

Double spiral

To make a double spiral, make a single spiral, but pull out an extra thread and leave it behind.

Then take the extra thread and spiral down the band in the opposite direction. Cool!

To finish

When the wrap is long enough, thread a bead (or two) onto the end. Make a knot, then trim the excess threads.

Remove the safety pin and replace with a cool hair clip. Ta-da! It's ready to clip on and wear.

Funky flip-flops

Here's a way of jazzing up your favourite flip-flops. You'll love showing off your style in the sun or on the beach.

Stuff you'll need!
- Flip-flops
- Cotton fabric, pom-poms, or ribbon
- Strong glue
- Scissors

1

Rip your fabric into 1cm (½in) wide strips. Make a small snip, then pull the strip off with your hands for a ragged effect.

Match the fabric to your flip-flops, or use a clashing colour for a bold look.

2

Loop each strip over the flip-flop strap and pull the ends through the loop to secure it in place.

Dip glass rims in orange juice, then into sugar or crushed sweets.

Prepare your mocktails in large jugs for a bigger group.

Cranberry Delight

- ¹/₂ glass apple juice
- ¹/₂ glass cranberry juice
- Strawberry to garnish

Jug of Pink Fizz

- 1 jug sparkling elderflower
- Squeeze of lime
- Splash of cranberry juice to make it pink!

Jug of St Clement's

- ¹/₂ jug orange juice
- ¹/₂ jug lemonade
- Orange and lime slices to garnish

67

Perfect popcorn

Popcorn is the perfect party snack and it's really easy to make. Add cheese or chocolate for an extra tasty treat that everyone will love.

Stuff you'll need!
- 1 tbsp sunflower oil
- 100g (3½oz) popping corn
- 40g (1½oz) cheese (and turmeric if you want)
- 60g (2oz) chocolate

1 ⚠ **Get an adult** to heat the oil in a saucepan. Stir in the popping corn and put the lid on. Wait for the popping to begin!

2 When the popping slows, shake the pan. Take off the heat when you hear just a few pops per second.

⚠ **Ask an adult** to melt the chocolate in a heat-proof bowl over boiling water.

Chocolate

⚠ Spread the popcorn on a baking tray. **Get an adult** to melt the chocolate, then drizzle it all over the popcorn. Leave it to cool.

You can add a pinch of turmeric for colour and flavour.

Cheese

Grate the cheese over the popcorn while it's warm. **Ask an adult** to put it under a hot grill for 30 seconds to melt the cheese. ⚠

68

The recipe makes
one large bowl
of popcorn.

Pizza hearts

These hearty pizzas are as delightful as they are delicious. For a treat everyone will love, let your guests choose their own toppings.

Stuff you'll need!

- 500g (1lb 2oz) flour, plus extra to dust
- A pinch of salt
- 4 tsp olive oil
- 2 tsp active dry yeast
- 360ml (12½fl oz) warm water
- Tomato passata
- Cheese
- A selection of toppings

Great topping ideas include mushrooms, salami, peppers, pineapple, ham – and anything else that takes your fancy!

1

Mix the flour, salt, and oil in a large bowl. In a small bowl, mix the yeast and warm water. Leave for five minutes. Slowly stir the yeast mixture into the flour mixture with a wooden spoon.

2

Put flour on your hands and work surface. Knead the dough for ten minutes, flattening it and folding it in half with your palm.

Ask an adult to help you knead the dough.

3

Put the dough back in the bowl and cover with cling film or a tea towel. Leave to rest for about an hour – until it's twice the size. After that, push your fist into the dough to knock out excess air and knead one more time.

Dough needs to rest in a warm place so it will rise.

4

 Roll the dough onto a floured surface and cut out heart shapes. Add the tomato passata, toppings, and cheese. **Ask an adult** to cook the pizzas in a 220°C (435°F) oven for 10 minutes, or until golden.

Ice-cream parlour

Ice cream is – quite literally – the coolest of all party snacks. Gather loads of tasty toppers and whip up your own sundae bar. Your friends will be so impressed!

Lay out bowls and spoons for everyone, and, of course, lots of ice-cream cones.

Fill bowls with different sweets, sprinkles, biscuits, and scrummy fruit.

Everyone can make their own dream sundae!

Don't forget yummy sauces, whipped cream, and cherries for the top!

Goodbye goodies

It's always nice to give a little something to your guests to thank them for coming to your party. Here are some ideas that will finish off your sleepover on the best note possible!

Sweet Treats

Retro-style sweetie jars make great vintage gifts. Fill them with loads of tasty, colourful delights!

Sundae Best

Create a pamper-time sundae in a plastic sundae glass. First add bath salts, then a bath pouf, and top with a small bath bead. To finish off, add an emery board and tie on a gift tag.

Funky Frames

Make a card photo frame and decorate with gemstones or stickers for each of your guests. They can put their favourite picture from the party inside it!.

Fashion Swag Bag

For a fashion-themed party bag, try hair clips, nail varnish, jewellery, and other fun, fashion stuff!

Tie a ribbon around for that final flourish.

Pamper Present

Why not do something different and give your gift at the *beginning* of a pamper party? Wrap a ribbon around a toothbrush and flannel so it's like your guests have arrived at a posh hotel!

Camping Rations

Fill a bag with camping-themed goodies, such as marshmallows, gummy worms, and a mini torch. For a personal touch, make a friendship bracelet for each guest and add it to the bag.

Rock Star Kit

Create a playlist with your favourite tunes so guests can rock out for the following few weeks.

Showtime Supplies

Print off an awards certificate for each guest for attending your party. Put it in a movie-themed party pack, filled with super-star stickers, a small bag of sweets, – and lots of popcorn, of course!

Sarah

Kayleigh

Write your guests' names on the labels.

Bath Salt Delight

Get a pretty jar and fill it with bath salts. Or why not add in the foot spa mix from page 22?

Templates

Copy these templates to help make the projects in the book.

How to use: All you have to do is use pencil to trace the templates onto thin paper. Turn the paper over, then draw over your pencil lines to transfer the pictures onto stiff paper or card. Cut out each shape and you'll have a template to draw around.

1 Fold a piece of card in half, and copy the template (right) onto it.

2 Cut out your heart shapes, smallest heart first.

3 Assemble the three hearts, one inside the other.

4 Tape string along the centre of the hearts, and then hang them up as decorations.

Place this edge against the fold in your card.

Hanging hearts pages 6-7

Heart bunting

Use the middle-sized template to make lots of hearts. Staple the hearts to a ribbon, and hang up as bunting.

Handbag invites
page 10

Write the invites straight onto the card. Coloured card works best, but make sure your guests can read your words.

⚠️ You may need to **ask an adult to help you** cut out the handles, as it's a bit fiddly.

Campout invites
page 8

Check out page 8 for all the instructions you need.

Don't forget to fold your card forwards along the dotted lines.

Eye mask
pages 38-39

If you are making eye masks with your guests, why not be super organised and make your templates before the party starts?

You can also use this template for your invitations on page 7.

Felt fun
pages 40-41

Mocktail straw decorations
pages 66-67

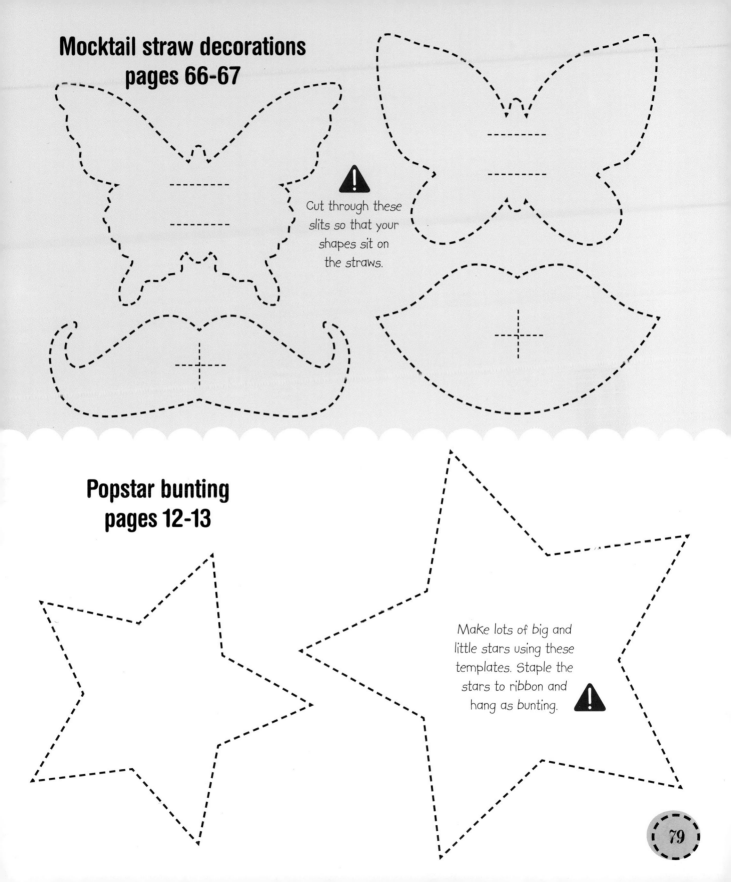

Cut through these slits so that your shapes sit on the straws.

Popstar bunting
pages 12-13

Make lots of big and little stars using these templates. Staple the stars to ribbon and hang as bunting.

79

Index

DK would like to thank

Dawn Sirett and Carrie Love for proofreading, Rosie Levine for jacket assistance, Kate Blinman for help with the recipes, and Charlotte Milner for illustrations.

With special thanks to the models: Lottie Burridge, Sahara Dosku, Lizzie Greenstreet, Jemimah Haque, Annabel Meadows, Ella Russell, Fatima Soltani, Sophie Tovell, Lucy Williams, Lilyann Yven-Dent, and Sophia Zaghetta.